JOUR

Acknowledgements

I have to start by thanking my wife Alisha for having patience with me while I was writing this book I know it has been hard on you due to my focus and drive to complete the book but I love and appreciate you.

Thank you to my mum Mrs Angela Williamson for pushing me to complete the book when I began to procrastinate and lose focus.

Dr Laura thank you for your support in the process of the writing may God continue to bless you and your ministry

Thiru thank you for insisting that we held fellowship because of that we were able to create for atmosphere for the spirit to dwell in. Thank you, Miss C Mango for listening to the voice of God and planting the seed in my spirit to write this book.

Mr M Corbally may God continue to bless and anoint your life you gave me your time by proof reading the book when you didn't have to but you did, words cannot express how grateful I am for your kindness.

I would like to thank God most of all because without you none of this would be possible.

Copyright

Scripture taken from the New King James Version. Copyright © 1982 by Thomas Nelson, Inc. Used by permission. All rights reserved.

Scripture quotations marked (NIV) are taken from the Holy Bible, New International Version ®, NIV ®. Copyright © 1973, 1978, 1984, 2011 by Biblica, Inc.™ Used by permission of Zondervan. All rights reserved worldwide. HYPERLINK "http://www.zondervan.com/"**www.zondervan.com** The "NIV" and "New International Version" are trademarks registered in the United States Patent and Trademark Office by Biblica, Inc.™

Scripture quotations marked (ESV) are from the ESV® Bible (The Holy Bible, English Standard Version®), copyright © 2001 by Crossway, a publishing ministry of Good News Publishers. Used by permission. All rights reserved.

Scriptures marked KJV are taken from the KING JAMES VERSION (KJV): KING JAMES VERSION, public domain.

All views in this book are solely of the author and the author alone.

It's the author choice not to put the enemy's name in capitals, as he does not wish to give the enemy any status or acknowledgment, despite knowing that this will cause grammatical errors.

Topics

1. Introduction

2. Why am I writing this?

3. My journey

4. Knowing your journey

5. Diverting from your journey

6. Experiences in our journeys prepare us for how God might use us

7. God can redirect your journey

8. Being aware of your path or journey in fellowship

9. Becoming spirit led

10. Losing people as we walk Gods new journey

11. Building your confidence in prayer

12. Finding someone who complements you and doesn't confine you

13. No denomination just togetherness in Christ

14. Building an atmosphere

15. Learn to forgive

16. Final thoughts

I have called the above 'topics' because I believe that to have a chapter, the first one must close before another can begin. However, with topics you can sit and discuss with each other in dialogue and learn and grow with each other by gaining understanding.

Introduction

The word 'journey' is defined as a noun (plural is 'journeys') – 'the act of travelling from one place to another' in the Oxford dictionary.

I believe that there are two types of journey, the first being a *physical* one whereby you (A): travel around the world or city to city or (B): from childhood into adulthood, the second being a spiritual journey in life. Both of these can happen separately and, every so often, they are woven into one.

People of the world tend to say I'm leaving to going a spiritual journey to find out who and what I am. Some find their answers quickly, whereas it takes others a lifetime. Regardless, if it takes you a lifetime or a few years, one thing is inevitable - we all must stand before God and answer to Him. As it is written in the Bible and states in *2 Corinthians 5:10 (KJV):*

"For we must all appear before the judgment seat of Christ; that every one may receive the things done in his body, according to that he hath done, whether it be good or bad."

Throughout the Bible there are records of men and women who have travelled on journeys in life. They all had one thing in common: they either knew their purpose, i.e. they knew what God wanted them to do and they fulfilled it. We see with some as their journey progressed that they learnt and understood what purpose God had for them. There were also those who God put on a journey but, when they tried to divert from their path, God soon straightened them out.

Why am I writing this?

This writing is all God and Spirit-led, while I was fasting in preparation for my baptism. My work colleagues and I had held fellowship, as we are all believers who were working that day. After the fellowship, I closed the fellowship in prayer but the atmosphere had already changed, as we had invited God's presence to be with us. As I was praying, it was as though I was looking out into an open plain and, once I opened my eyes, it took me a few seconds to get my bearings. My colleague turned to me and said: "You need to write a book." I laughed it off as a joke, then but she repeated it again - I realized that she was serious and I said "ok." Little did I know when I was driving home, God began to present me with: scriptures, the title of book, topics that I should write, how to lay it out and how to link what he was telling me to what I have experienced, so that when people read this book they can see God's work in people. Within God's people you are not alone - someone may have travelled the same path as you.

My Journey

We all have experienced one or maybe two or even all the topics that are in this book. I personally have experienced them all or have seen close friends and family go through them. Being in the Catholic Church from a young age, you just seem to just follow the structure. Every Sunday is the same besides, except they might change the hymns at Sunday mass, but it was almost robotic. I reached the point where I knew everything that the priest would say at every moment of the service. Because you don't know any better you just seem to just follow blindly. I left the Catholic Church after years and became lost in the world. At that age, I wanted to kick football and be with friends rather than go church. My brothers attended a Pentecostal church long before me as they used to go with my mum. I was hard headed and wanted to do other things. My first experience of a Pentecostal Church was when

I was, I think, 11 – 12 years of age.

I remember going in sitting there and realising that it is not as regimental. It felt as though it was free flowing, more relaxed and it was new and exciting to see so many young people bonding, having fun and enjoying themselves. An early memory that stands out for me was on a Sunday when I first saw and heard a woman speaking in tongues. It frightened me because I hadn't seen or heard that before, but only I seemed phased by it. I remember watching and trying to understand and make sense of it all. The next few years I found myself in and out of the church as young men do, till I turned my back on God and wasn't interested all. Going on a youth Christian camp brought me back to the Lord and being around young people again who oozed passion for Christ was amazing. Once again, I was learning about Christ, finding and discovering a new love for him. I first gave my life to God at that camp and I felt as though I personally was on the right track.

Lo and behold, just days after camp, I would experience things that I did not understand. I thought I couldn't talk to anyone about the things I was experiencing, that feeling of being alone. I got the courage to speak to someone and they explained to me that, once you accept Christ, your spiritual journey begins. They advised me on how to deal with certain things if they were to happen again. I am still going to church. I'm learning to pray but I never would pray out loud. Life begins to feel as though everything was on the right track. My first test and I turned my back on God: something happened to a good friend of mine and I couldn't understand why God would make this happen to him, as he comes from a very strong praying family. So, I turned back to my old ways of smoking, drinking, just being in the world. While quiet, I would at times read my Bible in my room or when I was alone. Friends would ask me if I still went to church and my response would be "yes" while, in the same breath, I'm smoking. This is all within a year of me being saved. The next camp date was arriving and I could not wait to go to see old faces and to catch up. I think it was a Tuesday night at camp and the Spirit of the Lord is was flooding in the room like a tsunami: all the children were praising and speaking in tongues. The Lord was in the place. I remember one of the young people taking the mic and saying, "If you believe in God and believe that he is your Lord and saviour, step forward and praise him." At that moment, I stood there quietly, not making a sound. A girl and I stood at the back while everyone was praising and we were so baffled about it. I was at the back thinking, "what are these people on, I don't feel nothing - I'm still upset at what happened to my friend." Someone approached and asked if I believed. I said, "Yes" and they coached me to go up to the pulpit. I went, standing there thinking, "Ok now what? Everyone around me is engulfed in the Holy Spirit and here I am, just here." After about an hour, it began to calm down and I felt as though I was left with more questions than answers. That latter part of the week, I gave myself to God again and promised to try harder. Once again, I'm home chilling with the lads. They go to smoke so I go with them and, as we are all just chatting, I'm offered to join them. I take it but my body rejects it almost instantly. It's a battle to walk the path that I know I need to travel. Confusion sets in and with it the thought, "do I struggle on this path or do I stray and do as my friends do?" I'm still not baptised or linked to a church, I just visit churches every Sunday. I remember turning to my best friend at church one day and saying, "There is something wrong! Something has changed in the church" and I never returned to worship at that church. I'm just doing my own thing reading and gaining my own understanding of the word with no fellowship, just me and my Bible.

I was experiencing things of a spiritual nature, but I had a fear of it going, as my confidence in the Lord was growing. I remember one evening, when I was praying and building an atmosphere in my room, asking God's presence to be in the room and the house. In the morning, two magpies were at the window tapping with their beaks, as if they were trying to enter. At that very moment, the Spirit of the Lord told me that I had cleared the room. They are now trying to enter physically because spiritually I had sealed the house. At this particular time in my life, I was so focused on God, people came to me asking for me to pray for them and God was giving me prayers especially for them. He was moving and shaping me into the man that he wanted me to be. Family and friends were now seeing a change and asking me what church I went to. My response was always the same: "I don't go to a set church. No matter what church I attend it always feels as though something is missing." I was reading and praying like a man on a mission and gaining understanding - I was beginning to stand firm in my faith. I had desire to, and the need to, fast for people who needed prayer. No one had told me how to fast, I was just doing it as God told me to. He told me that I needed to do a fast for myself. I heard him as he kept on telling me, but I did not listen. I continued to fast for others and the blessings were amazing.

Quietly, I remember going to a prayer meeting and everyone was praying out loud. I was praying but it was a silent prayer. To me it felt as though I was getting drowned out by everyone's prayer which was not the case, it was just how it felt. I was with my friend and he turned to me and said, "Do you remember when you told me that the church had changed and it's not the same and you cannot tell what's going on?" I replied, "Yes" and he continued, "well today at church the pastor stood up on the altar and said exactly what you had said four years ago." I was shocked, couldn't believe what he was telling me. How could I know something that was happening within the church before anyone else?

Many years down the line, I'm still very strong in my faith and spirituality getting stronger in my stance of my faith. I cannot put my finger on it and, although I'm not praying as much, my faith is my foundation. I'm back in the world clubbing, drinking but people still ask for me to pray for them and I do it. When I'm asked to pray, my spirit man rises up and overcomes the flesh and I do what I need to do in prayer. Once it's dealt with, I'm back to the worldly living. This is me for the next few years.

No one ever hears my prayers; I pray silently because I don't want anyone to hear my prayers. Until my partner tells me that we need to pray, I'm shy. She is praying confidently out loud, articulating her words so eloquently as I'm praying quietly. The next evening, we prayed again and I finally opened my mouth and let my words be free for the first time. I prayed out loud: it was a short prayer, but I beat the shyness that was holding me back all this time. The more I pray out loud, the more confident I'm becoming in prayer.

I feel as though I am moving to another level within my faith. God tells me once again that I must fast for myself. This time, I heed his words and I fast for a week. I feel so blessed constantly being in God's company praying, reading and worshipping. God tells me to do a 30-day fast but, after week two, it's starting to become a battle. The devil is really attacking me. I remember being at my mothers and breaking down crying like a new born baby. I felt heavy and just wanted to break the fast, but my partner and my mom prayed for me and I felt a heavy burden on my shoulder lift off me. I felt renewed and refreshed - I had a new lease of life.

Being in church so many times, I had the pastor call me out and tell me "What are you waiting for? You know what you need to do." At this present day now, I have now been baptised after years of being stubborn. Back then I thought that, even though I gave my life to the Lord already verbally, why would I need to get baptised? But that was just my lack of understanding talking. I am still helping, advising and praying for those who need it with the Lord God leading me.

This is just me giving you a small insight of my journey. I could write so much more. No matter what, God has always been on my side. I haven't given full details of my experiences, but I have tried to show you how my journey started and is continuing to this date.

Some of the chapters in this book I will be discussing are:

Knowing your journey - Now that my journey is with Christ, I try to gain an understanding of the gifts that He has bestowed upon me. I am learning on my journey that, after each step, He opens another door and with each step I grow.

Diverting from your journey - I, like most, have diverted from the journey and path that God put me on, so many times I have diverted.

Experiences in our journeys prepare us for how God might use us – what I have experienced has helped me grow spiritually, and it has also helped me to help those around me that might be going through the same thing.

God can redirect your journey – when I was going away

from my path/journey God redirected me, put me back on track and it's where I have remained.

Being aware in your path of fellowship – I know who I am in Christ. I am confident in my faith that if something seems off, then more than likely something is wrong.

Becoming spirit led – doing what God tells me to do without a second thought. If I'm led to support or pray for someone, I must do.

Building your confidence in prayer – changing from a shy person in praying, to a man that will pray anywhere and at any given time.

Losing people as we walk God's new journey – many of the people I used to talk and chill with when I was in the world

I no longer see or hear from.

Building an atmosphere – having an environment where the Holy Spirit can dwell.

Knowing your journey

A man that knew His path, His journey, was Jesus - from the time he was a child, he knew exactly the plan. He knew His journey in and with God at the temple as a child, when He was speaking with the elders listening and asking questions. At such a young age this was unheard of, but when God is with you and you work within your chosen path it doesn't matter who, where or what. People will have to listen and hear what you have to say. Luke 2:41-52 is the story of young Jesus in the temple.

How do we know our journey? The only way is by praying and dwelling in the company of God. There are not many people that know their journey in Christ beforehand. For almost all of us, we only know our journey once we are beginning to make steps towards it. So how do we know we are on a journey of

God and not of flesh?

I am reminded of a scripture: Romans 12:2 (NIV) Do not conform to the pattern of this world, but be transformed by the renewing of your mind. Then you will be able to test and approve what God's will is—His good, pleasing and perfect will. By not abiding in the flesh but in the spirit and by God's grace, learning to separate the desires of the flesh from the desire of the spirit, only then can the Spirit of the Lord work within you and lead you on your journey.

The question I asked earlier was: "So how do we know we are on a journey of God and not of flesh?" What I meant by this is that the journey within God is a spiritual journey and the journey of the flesh is a worldly journey. If we are to know our spiritual journey, then we need to know GOD. To first know GOD, we need to first accept him in our lives. Then secondly we need to do as Jesus did, the man that had no sin but He felt fit that he needed to get baptised.

In John 3:5 (NIV) Jesus answered, "Very truly I tell you, no one can enter the kingdom of God unless they are born of water and the Spirit. ⁶ Flesh gives birth to flesh, but the Spirit gives birth to spirit."

John is teaching us that we are to be born of water to enter the kingdom of heaven and the only way to do that is by baptism. I believe that it is a symbolic action for us to be born of spirt renewed in our flesh by accepting Jesus Christ as our Lord and Saviour. So, as we submit our lives to God he will give us directions through dreams and visions. So many times, you can see that God gives men and woman visions and dreams to prepare them for their journeys.

In Amos 3:7 (NIV) it states: - 'Surely the Sovereign LORD does nothing without revealing his plan to his servants the prophets.'

I like this verse because it clearly states that God is always one step ahead of us. Sometimes, before even we know it, he puts his plan in motion; he will tell one of his servants - it could be in church or from a loved one - that he has a plan for you. They tell us what has been revealed to them and, low and behold, it starts to manifest in us and we are already on the journey that he has set out for us.

ACTS 2:17 (NIV) states: 'In the last days, God says I will pour out my Spirit on all people. Your sons and daughters will prophesy, your young men will see visions, your old men will dream dreams.'

If we submit to God, it is written that he will pour his spirit unto us. If we believe, have faith, if we are steadfast in our faith, then we can be spiritually confident for God to give us direction on our journey. I don't see how he wouldn't let us know our journey or path. It would be as if we are about to enter a labyrinth at night, and we walk in without any idea where we are going, just endlessly walking and turning left and right without realising where we are going. With God, we can enter that same said labyrinth at night, and He becomes the light which brightens up the way ahead of us. He is the voice inside us that is telling us when to turn and when to walk straight and in the end, we reach the end of the labyrinth. To know your journey is to trust the Lord without fear or hesitation. Many of us know Him, but we are not listening and have become lost in the labyrinth, searching with no clear way ahead. To know God and to listen to God is to become Spirit-led, which I shall go into more detail with in another chapter.

Diverting from your journey

Adam and Eve knew God's law but they chose to not follow God's instructions. There are consequences and repercussions. God could have easily stepped in and said, "Eve, what are you doing? You know my law" but he allowed their free will to take place and they lost their place in grace.

Adam was put on his path/journey. He had to take care of the Garden of Eden and the animals in it. You could argue that Eve never heard from God, but the instructions given to her were from Adam as it states that God spoke to Adam. Nonetheless, he should have known better. For all his troubles God then made his path/journey a long and tedious one.
(Genesis 2:4-3:24 - read and see how they were diverted from their path /journey.)

How does that mirror us compared to this day and age? Easy! Think of a time when you were in God's grace; everything was sweet and for a moment or a split second you lost your way and the road became long and rough, tedious, never ending.

You cannot understand or figure out how and when it happened but you unknowingly strayed away from God. You feel as though He is getting further and further away but, in all reality, He never left you. Your free will made you step away, your free will made you blind, but He is ever loving and ever forgiving. We just need to repent and seek His grace again and He will forgive us if our hearts are sincere. We blame him for things that have nothing to do with Him, meaning we blame Him for the bad things that happen in this world and to us. Not realising the person we need to blame is satan, as he tries to manipulate us into thinking that God is the reason for the negative things that happen, by instilling that one question that many use: "If there is a God, why does He allow bad things to happen in the world?" In life and during our journey, people for some reason put God and satan on the same pedestal.

Sounds crazy but people do it and it gives satan power over them. The moment they realise and open their eyes, that God is the alpha and the omega and satan has no power over you, once you accept God in your life. You will see that God created the angels, so how can they be on the same pedestal? A creation can never be on the level as the creator. Satan himself had a path and a journey, but though he was the mightiest of all angels, it wasn't enough. He wanted more, and thus his path and journey changed. He wants us to be his, he wants the praises and the glory but we need to be strong and not give him anything. He doesn't deserve anything (the praises and glory.)

Losing people as we walk God's new journey

I am reminded of the song lyrics "I can't go back. I won't go back to the place I used to be". Dwell where you used to be? Are you the same person spiritually now than before God came? The environments, the social groups that consumed your life, you slowly lose interest in them. Imagine two circles linked in the middle:

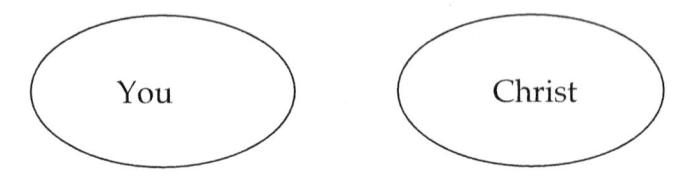

(You)   (Christ)

The section on the left is the world (YOU) living in sin with not a care spiritually. The second circle is Christ.

As we learn about Christ, He enters our lives and we begin to change. The illustration below shows where God enters us as we learn about Him as we read the Bible and pray. It creates an inner circle as shown in the illustration. As we begin to learn, we become warm and it is our decision whether we stay in the world, be warm or be hot in Christ. With both circles linked together, we can see that there is now 3 parts to it, Part 1, Part 2 and Part 3.

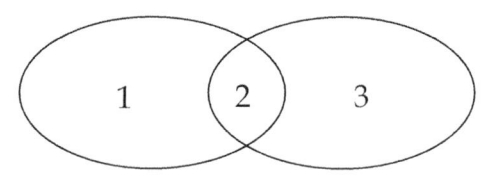

Part 1 is the world. Part 2 is where we are starting to know God or we have been in Him. Part 3 we have slipped back into wanting worldly things. Part 3 is being fully submerged in Christ. This Bible scripture says that we cannot serve two masters:

Luke 16:13 (NIV) - "No one can serve two masters. Either you will hate the one and love the other, or you

will be devoted to the one and despise the other. You cannot serve both God and money."

We cannot be in Christ and the world. We need to be in the world, not of the world. When we are in Christ, He will confiscate things from our lives so that we flourish in His grace. He puts us in situations to test us, things that He knows we can deal with, but we have to find that inner strength and faith to come through it, so that we stand strong and remain in PART 3.

At times, we are put in a situation and we struggle to discover that hidden strength and faith and we slip. We become lost, so we become a part of the world, but we still hold onto Christ. Unbeknown to ourselves, we are serving two masters, but we never truly go back to the phase of PART 1, as God has already changed us. We need to find and execute the strength and plan that he has instilled in us. Yes, God could sort it out for us, but how will we learn if every obstacle we reach we never learn to climb over and conquer? It's like a child always trying to climb a wall, but each time he tries he falls, but he never sees the box at the side of the wall, because he is too preoccupied and has tunnel vision in trying to get over the wall. He is blind to the fact that nearby is something that can help him. Until he stops and refocuses, only then will he notice the box. It's as if a light bulb goes off in his head and he can conquer the wall by using the box. This is a perfect example to show how God works. We get so caught up in a situation and we ask God for assistance, but if we stop and refocus, we will see that He has already given us what we need.

Matthew 7:7 (KJV) - "Ask, and it shall be given you; seek, and ye shall find; knock, and it shall be opened unto you".

This is why we lose people who are of the world - because we as people can be like crabs in a barrel. When you try to get out, change yourself, the others try and pull you back in. God's will eliminates people and desires from ourselves so we remain on course.

How many of us have lost close friends, people who were even more close to us than our own families because we decided to walk a new path with God. We wanted to break the mould and get out of the cycle that we had created for ourselves. Some people don't like change, they don't like routines to be broken, and they don't like to see people leave them behind. This happens. It's a fact and yes it will hurt, but is your journey to salvation yours or friends?

This is a life journey that is beginning to end and God's journey starting to begin.

Scenario: let us build a picture. You have a close friend. Day in, day out you are together. You do everything together; you have grown and experienced the same things. Then one day you turn to him and say "I want to be a Christian and follow God's way." This statement is going to test your friendship. Your friend's reaction could go either way. He/she could say "I am happy for you." and then try to find out what made you come to the decision. They in turn could ask, "How long have you been feeling like this?" Why didn't you speak to them about? they might want to follow and give God a try. On the other hand they laugh at you and tell you to shut up.

If you have a friend like the first person, then you are truly blessed by God's grace because he has given you someone with understanding, someone who will not judge you but one who wants to learn more about the things that you are involved in. Those people are a blessing in our lives. These people will be ones that when you slip, they will pick you up and support you in good and bad. They see your growth and they want to grow alongside you.

The friends that laugh at you and try to put you down, those friends are the people that we pray for the most. Those are the ones that mock you like they mocked Christ. They dismiss your decision as the disciples doubted that Christ was resurrected until they saw him for himself.

John 20:29 (ESV) - 'Jesus said to him, "Have you believed because you have seen me? Blessed are those who have not seen and yet have believed.'

The above scripture shows and tells us that, as man, we have weakness in faith but to walk in Christ is to walk in the unseen, not the seen.

2 Corinthians 5: 6 – 8 (NKJV) - 'So we are always confident, knowing that while we are at home in the body we are absent from the Lord. For we walk by faith, not by sight. We are confident, yes, well pleased rather to be absent from the body and to be present with the Lord.'

Sometimes the devil will use your friends to distract you from your goal, because one soul gained by God is lost to satan. As God's army strengthens, satan's army deteriorates. He doesn't want you to walk the path. He wants you for Himself, so that's why when you step out and you make that decision your battle begins from that moment.

Some say that it's a lonely journey but it's not, because God is always with you. Remember you just have to call on His name and He will answer. Yes, it will hurt when the ones that we classed as brothers and sisters abandon you, but you lose one and gain so many. More in the fellowship of Christ if they loved you for you, then they would support your decision and not ridicule you. I dare you to step out of the box and see who is still with you when you break the mould. To be fair, it might be swings and roundabouts as those same friends that ridiculed you might one day find themselves coming to you for support. Beware of the wolves in sheep clothing, the friends that come back just to try and tear you down so they can say, "I TOLD YOU SO". Pray to God to make your eyes open, not your physical, but your spiritual eyes open.

Proverbs 18:24 (ESV) - 'A man of many companions may come to ruin, but there is a friend who sticks closer than a brother.'

Just a verse for you to mediate on: cling onto Christ and you will never come to ruin ,but hold onto friends or family who don't support and ridicule you and it might bring your downfall.

Experiences in our journeys prepare us for how God might use us.

Have you ever just spoken to someone and just through them hearing and listening, you can fully recognize and appreciate everything that they say?

2 Timothy 3:16 (NIV) - 'All Scripture is God-breathed and is useful for teaching, rebuking, correcting and training in righteousness.'

Within our journeys, we each individually go through trials which unknowingly are preparing us for Christ. Experiencing things in our life enables us to relate to people around us in and out of the church. Most young people feel as though they cannot relate to anyone within the church, because of either fear or misunderstanding - automatically thinking that if they open their mouth, they will get Bible bashed or have Christ forced down their throat or be judged.

So, what do they do? They bottle things up and let it out in a negative way. The greatest gift we as Christians can give people is a listening ear, just listen, be impartial and don't judge.

Proverbs 18:13 (NIV) - 'To answer before listening, that is folly and shame.'

Listen to them, give feedback and respond appropriately. You might have experienced the same things as them. Please don't make it seem like a competition. That means when you say things like, "well when I dealt with it I did this, I did that." We as Christians seriously have to be more understanding, so why not say things like "I have experienced some of the same things." Therefore, giving the intended young or older person time to respond and ask you the question, "what did you do?"

By doing this, it makes it better received and not as though it's a competition or one upmanship. Trust me, people out there are yearning for a person that they can open up to, let their guard down with and seek advice from. The trouble occurs when knowing when to talk and when to listen. By listening, you can hear the struggles of those that are pouring themselves out to you. Yes, you have gone through it so you can relate and reason with them; help them to grow and by helping them you are also helping yourself. One man that had to go and experience things before he could go and help his people was Moses. Do you think that he would have been able to deal with the things that he did while he was still living in the palace? When he stood in front of the pharaoh and the pharaoh's wizards turned their staffs into snakes, if he had not dealt with the snakes while he was out in the wildness and gained knowledge of how to deal with it. Then surely, he would have failed, but no, God gave him training out there farming. Experiencing things unknown to him, God was preparing him, instilling things deep within him so when he came across it, he would know exactly what to do.

From **Exodus 2,** it details the journey of Moses and everything that he had done and seen to make him into the man that God wanted him to be. He may not have understood why God chose him but that is not for him to know. Though he had reservations at times, he still followed through with what God wanted him to do. During the journey in Christ you are continuously learning, continuously maturing, but have you ever thought everything that we experience is not only for our own edification but for those in and out of Christianity?

God will redirect your journey

How many of us are running? How many of us are running because God asked us to do something? You begin to walk in Christ and He wants you to accomplish those things that He has already ordained into your life. With all this in front of us, we allow a seed of doubt to enter us which starts to manifest itself and we run. Not running as you run away or run a race, but more that you ignore his word. We turn our back because we do not want to do it. We all have done it once or twice in our lives, maybe.

Psalm 37:23-24 (NIV) - 'The LORD makes firm the steps of the one who delights in him; though he may stumble, he will not fall, for the LORD upholds him with his hand.'

God may ask you to approach a stranger and talk to them. He may have told you to pray for someone that you are not keen on, or he told you give someone something. God will let you disobey him, because he wants to see who is truly for him or who talks a good old game. Naturally it's human nature to question, it is part and parcel of our free will. What we seem not to understand is that when God has had enough of the disobedience, he will put you back on track. A man that tried to change his journey in the Bible is Jonah.

Jonah 1-2 (NIV) - 'The word of the LORD came to Jonah son of Amittai: "Go to the great city of Nineveh and preach against it, because its wickedness has come up before me." But Jonah ran away from the LORD and headed for Tarshish. He went down to Joppa, where he found a ship bound for that port. After paying the fare, he went aboard and sailed for Tarshish to flee from the

LORD.'

I won't give you all the scripture, but you can search for it. Here we see that God is always watching. I recall my mother using an old saying: "you can run but you cannot hide" - this comes to mind when I read that scripture. Our free will can at times be our undoing; as Jonah disobeyed, we do it and don't realise it. For example, God could tell you that He wants you to be a pastor, but you think that you are unable to step into such a big, respectable role within God's church. So you sit back and don't tell anyone that God has given an addition to your journey. Years pass and you still haven't fulfilled your path and, when we think we have hidden away from it or even forgot all about the message that God has given, God tells the pastor or a member in your fellowship and they prophesize and tell you what God has already told you - once again, proving that you cannot hide. Your brethren begin to pray, help and support you to walk on the path that you are supposed to be walking on.

Acts 16 records Paul's Vision of the Man of Macedonia. Here Paul is travelling and unable to speak the word of God. Earlier on in his journey, he was preaching and spreading the word of God. As he travelled to the different cities, the Spirit of the Lord stopped him. It was only when he had a vision that he was sent on his journey and he knew his destination. So you see, Paul thought that he could go to any city, but his journey was changed by the Spirit of the Lord. So when we are in Christ, we need to understand that the journey is not ours but at God's grace. Some doors are not of God's will and are not meant for you to enter: God closes it for your protection. Our heavenly father knows everything past and in existence and he knows if you're on a path that will lead you to danger.

God will redirect our everyday lives and we wouldn't even know it until we have reached halfway on his planned destination. We can set a plan for ourselves and God will have other ideas for us and he will close that door and open another door.

Isaiah 22:22 (NIV) - 'I will place on his shoulder the key to the house of David; what he opens no one can shut, and what he shuts no one can open.'

You pray to God asking for a way forward to better yourself in your career. He helps and guides you to the place where you are supposed to be, but little did you know that the step in the right direction has many more doors for you to enter. On the other hand, there are times when the door that has opened doesn't look as glamorous. Subsequently, we proceed with it for a while and decide to turn our backs on it and go searching for greener pastures - not realising that, if we had just stayed put, it was everything plus more than we had prayed for. Sometimes the tunnel might be long, but the journey is what makes us into stronger people in the fellowship of Christ. So we leave thinking that we have found greener pastures, only to realise that we have jumped right out of the pan into the fire. Falling on our knees we are praying and asking God, "why has this happened?" but unknown to us, we stood on the right path. Nonetheless, God will not leave us there...he will hear our prayers and our cries - he will put us back into the position we were supposed to be. We have just made it harder for ourselves when the original path he put us on might not have looked glamorous, but it was the easiest route.

On the other hand, we could be stuck in a dead end job working like a robot, not being satisfied so we ask God "is this the life that you have in store for me?" - in time he answers your prayers. Blessings are coming to your life, you are able to move job and now, you finally received your blessing. That past door is now closed, but the new door that he opened has many doors opened to us. Just because it doesn't happen straight away doesn't mean that things are not already in motion.

Matthew 7:7-8 (NIV) - 'Ask and it will be given to you; seek and you will find; knock and the door will be opened to you. For everyone who asks receives; the one who seeks finds; and to the one who knocks, the door will be opened.'

Being aware on your path or journey within fellowship

What is fellowship? According to the Oxford dictionary, Fellowship is described as 'friendly association, especially with people who share one's interests. '

1 John 1:7 New International Version (NIV) - 'But if we walk in the light, as he is in the light, we have fellowship with one another, and the blood of Jesus, his Son, purifies us from all sin.'

Fellowship is what we should do as Christians. We come together as one as the verse says, "If we walk in the light as he is the light, we have fellowship with one another." If we all share the same interest, the same desire and the passion, why is it so hard for us to get along?

When I say being aware in your path or journey within fellowship, I mean sticking to God's plans for you within the fellowship. How many of us have been diverted from our journey because we listened to fellow members, or even the pastor? It might come as a shock to you, but it is true. How many of us have been given a message from God and when we bring it to the pastor, he says "no. I think you should do this." Now I am NOT saying this happens in every church, but it does happen.

I used to have a saying that I always use to use when people asked me why am I not a member of a Church. The quote went like this: "fellowship is good but can lead to dictatorship which leads to demonization of your church, meaning that by being dictated to or being the dictator how can you hear God's word? How can you follow God's plan when you want control and enforce your word, and your word becomes the last final word?"

Example 1 - God gives you a message that you should have a role within the church and you go to the pastor. You say the Lord has spoken to me and he has given me this message, and he turns to you and he says "no I think you should do this."

Example 2 - God gives the pastor a message that a person is to give a message to the congregation, but the pastor doesn't tell that person, because he thinks that another brother or sister will be able to deliver the message better than the person God said should give the message. Has he not diluted the word? Yes, the person may be delivering the word but the word doesn't have the same punch as it should have, because he didn't do as he was told.

The scripture says: *'**James 1:22-23** - 'Do not merely listen* *to the word, and so deceive yourselves. Do what it says. Anyone who listens to the word but does not do what it says is like someone who looks at his face in a mirror [24] and, after looking at himself, goes away and immediately forgets what he looks like.'*

Proverbs 16:20 (NIV) - 'Whoever gives heed to instruction prospers, and blessed is the one who trusts in the LORD.'

Try to stay away from the inner turmoil that you may or may not come across.

Job 1:6 (NIV) - 'One day the angels came to present themselves before the LORD, and Satan also came with them.'

This shows that when God calls, the devil will try and dwell where God himself is, so don't be fooled. He will enter your sanctuary and plant seeds in people and watch them manifest. You see it in the church. The church is immersed; the Holy Spirit flowing freely, there is always an anointing on the people. Church is overflowing then next thing down the line there is only a hand full of people left. Stay strong in Christ and you cannot go wrong, stay wrapped in His grace, stay convicted in His Spirit and the devil will never get a foothold. Remove all seeds that he has planted like a gardener removes weeds from his land. Be attentive - support and help build each other up. Though you are in fellowship, you need to have your own relationship with God - you need to be firm in what God tells you:

John 1:1 - '(ESV) In the beginning was the Word, and the Word was with God, and the Word was God.'

So if God is talking to you, telling you what he wants you to do within your fellowship you need to take heed and listen. You should pray on it and go to the pastors or church leaders and say: "God has told me the job that he wants me to do." Your pastor or church leaders should immediately start praying; even better, they should fast and pray on what you have told them. The pastor or church leaders are the shepherds of Christ's flock, so God will and should affirm in them what you have told them. By each one of us doing as God says without questioning and without disobeying, the church should flourish and the Holy Spirit will once again be rampant in the church.

Throughout the Bible in the Old Testament and the New Testament, you can see that God himself has warned us about false prophets. There are people that will act as though they are holy and righteous. They will try and prophesize on your life, proclaiming the message is from God when it is not. They preach false messages.

Deuteronomy 18: 21 – 22 - '(KJV) And if thou say in thine heart how shall we know the word which the lord hath not spoken, when a prophet speaketh in the name of the lord, if the thing follow not, nor come to pass, that is the thing which the lord hath not spoken, but the prophet hath spoken it presumptuously thou shalt not be afraid of him.'

Here, you can see that God is telling His people how to know if a prophet is true or not. He is telling His people that if a man prophecies and it does not come true, then he is a false prophet. So why do we continually, as God's people, hang onto false prophet's words? God himself in Deuteronomy told you how to know the real from the fake. Do not be blind to these people, but remember the Bible is how you interpret it. Whenever you are told a word given by a preacher, you should always go and read and get your own understanding.

Matthew 7:15 (KJV) - 'watch out for false prophets. They come to you in sheep clothing, but inwardly they are ferocious wolves.'

Jesus also himself notified us of false prophets in:

Matthew 24:24-25 (NIV) - 'For false messiahs and false prophets will appear and great signs and wonders to deceive, if possible, even the elect. See I have told you ahead of time.'

We have been warned, people; please keep your spiritual eyes open and focused on God - join in fellowship, but remember to remain steadfast in Christ. A question that I have thought about for a while is: "If God gave prophets in the Old Testament information and Jesus has warned us about false prophets. Who is accountable for you being diverted from God's original path for you?" Fellowship can be an amazing and wonderful experience, when you are in fellowship and its right for you. Then you will burst open like a blossoming, beautiful flower. A gardener will tend to his land before he plants his seeds or young plants. This is like God working in you, when you accept him, he starts affecting you. Your life changes, it can be slow changes but it starts and you don't even realise when it happens. He puts you in a place which is suited for you to grow. We are young, learning...experiencing new things. Fellowship within church is our soil. Like a plant we are there to grow from participating in fellowship. As we progress in fellowship, our roots go deep and we begin to grow inward spiritually. The more we embrace God the more we grow, even when we have blossomed and are filled with

the Holy Spirit, we still continue to grow.

Becoming Spirit led

What is being Spirit led?

Spirit led is about following your spirit once you have heard from God. You begin to hear from God once you commit yourself to strive in his journey. It takes time to hear from God - you need to build a connection with him and not allow your mind to influence your heart to stop you. Following your spirit engages your heart; it is being satisfied with the glory of God and puts your mind - which is one of the ultimate battle grounds - into submission. Some say it's that little voice that you hear when you are about to do something wrong, or begin to head in the wrong direction, knowing that you shouldn't be going that way.

So many people in the Bible are Spirit led; the men in the Old Testament that God himself used to accomplish many duties where led by the Spirit. In the New Testament, the men and women that followed Christ where also Spirit led. Christ himself was Spirit led on many occasions in His life, but it is through Christ that we have access to the Holy Spirit. Through the Holy Spirit, God can set us tasks to follow, but sometimes it can be a test to see whether or not we have completely let go and are whole heartedly willing to be led by him, no matter how tedious the task might seem.

John 4:24 (ESV) - 'God is spirit, and those who worship Him must worship in spirit and truth.'

So, to worship God is to worship in spirit and truth. We can go years without actually worshiping God with our spirit due to becoming robots and followers, not of God's word, but of the man in the pulpit. Many people are caught up in the pastor saying that this, pastor says that, but I question and say: what does GOD's Spirit say to you? How long will you ignore that voice? How long will you allow the world to suppress the Spirit that Jesus gave us access to?

Jesus is the bridge that connects us to the Holy Spirit. It's like having two magnets and holding them together. You feel the energy drawing, pulling them close and, as you get closer to that energy, it becomes stronger until the magnets are stuck together. That is symbolic of Christ working in our lives. Yes, on the other hand the magnets can push each other away but that's because, in life, God is always there and it is satan who is in the middle that is keep us from reaching our true destination. Once you turn one magnet around they are attracted to each other, so this is also symbolic of your turning your life around and allowing Jesus to take charge and being led by His Spirit to bring you closer to God.

The disciples are perfect examples of being led by their spirit in turn making a connection with God's Spirit through Jesus. In fact, all of them were in different stages of their lives and Jesus inspired them, just like the magnets that have two different energies pulling them together, they were pulled to Christ. Christ in a few words had activated the human spirit needed to once again be one with God. Jesus told them to stop what they were doing and to follow him and some, without a second thought, dropped what they were doing and followed him. I believe, at that moment, their spiritual eye overcame their worldly eye and they were captivated by the grace of God.

As the bible says:

2 Corinthians 5:7 (KJV) - 'For we walk by faith, not by sight.'

We as followers need to stop looking with our eyes and look with our spiritual eyes, so we may become led by the Spirit. We need to fix our eyes on Christ and have complete faith in him. The moment we take our eyes off Him, we sink as the disciple did in the scripture when he was walking on water and he took his eyes off Jesus and sank.

I believe becoming Spirit led is the result of the foundation of our unwavering faith in Christ.

When you do not understand the situation, when you do not understand the motive, blessed are those who follow through and listen to what has been told. Your faith will instill in you and your spirit should tell you, God will not lead you in a wrong direction. Even when the journey might seem as though you have taken a wrong turn, there is a reason you are there; for example, you might be there as a beacon of light in which the land is dark. You might be there because God wants to train you, so you are ready to do his work.

Acts 17:8 (NIV) - 'He said to them: "It is not for you to know the times or dates the Father has set by his own authority. But you will receive power when the Holy Spirit comes on you; and you will be my witnesses in Jerusalem, and in all Judea and Samaria, and to the ends of the earth." '

The Holy Spirit is already promised to us. In many verses, Jesus promised us that we will receive the Holy Spirit, as long as we obey Him, and to obey Him is to be led by Him.

Romans 10:17 (KJV) - 'So then faith cometh by hearing, and hearing by the word of God.'

Take the time to listen as much as you ask in prayer. We can be so eager to talk that we forget to listen. The more we listen, the more we will witness the miraculous works of the Lord. Use your foundation which is faith to engage your spirit to be attracted to Jesus and then to be led by him, just like the disciples.

Building your confidence in prayer

When we pray, we are actively making a connection with God; we are bridging the gap between the heavenly realm and the earthly realm. We see a lot of people praying confidently out loud when we start to walk in Christ. It can be quite daunting to pray out loud. We question ourselves and say: "I do not know what to say," forcing ourselves to pray a silent prayer. We have all experienced this, especially if you have never been around praying people. I was always one to pray quietly, never wanted anyone to hear what I was saying as some people pray so eloquently.

I remember one experience when I was at prayer meeting and everyone was praying, I stood there and was praying quietly, and it felt as if I was getting drowned out - as if I was getting swallowed up and my prayer wasn't getting heard. You might find that when you pray, you might get random thoughts that distract you. These happen because satan doesn't want you to make that spiritual connect with God - and satan will put a seed of doubt in you; you will tell yourself that you cannot pray, because you cannot articulate as those around you do so sit or stand there quietly, listening to others when you should be praying.

Have the faith to understand that when you pray God is hearing you. The same way that you can pray quietly is the same way you can pray out loud. The same words you say quietly - just open your mouth, but too many times we watch and listen to others pray and we become disheartened and we beat ourselves up, because we think we cannot pray as good as them.

WHO DETERMINES WHAT A GOOD PRAYER IS?

When we are new to the faith and spirituality of Christ we learn that prayer is an important part:

Psalm 145:18 (NKJV) - 'The LORD is near to all who call upon Him, To all who call upon Him in truth.'

The sooner you get rid of your nervousness, embarrassment or shyness that people might be listening to your words, the sooner you will grow in prayer. As you read, you will see that even the disciples did not know how to pray and it was Jesus who taught them with the Lord's prayer in:

Luke 11 (NIV) - 'And it came to pass, that, as he was praying in a certain place, when he ceased, one of his disciples said unto him, Lord, teach us to pray, as John also taught his disciples.[2] And he said unto them, when ye pray, say, Our Father which art in heaven, Hallowed be thy name. Thy kingdom come. Thy will be done, as in heaven, so in earth.[3] Give us day by day our daily bread.[4] And forgive us our sins; for we also forgive every one that is indebted to us. And lead us not into temptation; but deliver us from evil.'

We are happy to pray the Lord's Prayer loud and proud, but when it comes to things that are close to us and personal to us we can be quite shy around people, because we don't want to be judged about what we have said in our prayers:

Matthew 6:6 (NKJV) - 'But you, when you pray, go into your room, and when you have shut your door, pray to your Father who is in the secret place; and your Father who sees in secret will reward you openly.'

Here in the scripture, you can see that it clearly states that the strongest prayer you can do is when you are alone in a quiet room and it's just you and God. Start to build a prayer life at home: pray, be in God presence and just because someone can pray for long, doesn't mean that your short prayer is not heard.

Matthew 6:7 (NKJV) - 'And when you pray, do not use vain repetitions as the heathen do. For they think that they will be heard for their many words.'

Do not be concerned of those around you, but be concerned with what you are saying to God. Sometimes, we may not understand where the words we are saying are coming from. It might even shock you at what you have said, but ultimately it is you having a conversation with God - sometimes our needs and want are vocalised even when, at many other times, we would have kept them to ourselves, but with God, we share everything - nothing can be hidden from him.

Romans 8:26 (NKJV) - 'Likewise the Spirit also helps in our weaknesses. For we do not know what we should pray for as we ought, but the Spirit Himself makes intercession for us with groaning's which cannot be uttered.'

So don't be alarmed as, when we pray, our spirit man takes over from our flesh and a spiritual connection is made. God will hear and grant you what you need as long as you have faith. I have a saying: *"PRAYER WITHOUT FAITH IS MEANINGLESS."*

You have to be unwavering in your faith. Your faith should be the corner stone for your spiritual journey as your faith becomes stronger and your prayer life becomes a part of your daily life. God will move in your life; you will hear from him, he will give you visions, dreams...you will slowly learn what it is he wants you do to. It could be as simple as saying. "Father God in heaven, Thank you for waking me up in the morning. Thank you for allowing me to see another day," It is a simple but honest statement to God on the blessing that he has given you; you woke up in your sane mind and are able to see another day.

Proverbs 27 (NKJV) - 'Do not boast about tomorrow, For you do not know what a day may bring forth.'

Say what comes to your mind or your heart; tell God your heart's desires and tell God your burdens. There is nothing too small or big that you cannot share with him. Your faith is your foundation. The stronger and deeper the foundation, the bigger building blocks, the bigger the grace God shall pour on you. Yes, it can be daunting to pray in front of the people, but the more you do it, the more confidence you will achieve. The more confidence you have in prayer, the greater connection you have with God and the more you will be able to be an agent of God. Remember: everyone is concentrating on their own prayer and if someone has something to say about how you pray, take no heed as that's how you felt and no flesh (person) has the authority to judge your words to God. Do not be scared in prayer, but be glad in it.

Finding someone who complements you and doesn't confine you.

God presented this topic to me as I was reflecting on my life experience, my marriage and others around me. I now realise that we as people are too quick to stay in a situation of convenience. Instead of acquiring what could be ours if you made God make the decision in this matter. The word 'complement' is defined as 'a thing that contributes extra features to something else in such a way to improve or emphasize its quality' - according to the Oxford dictionary. The word 'confines' means 'to keep or restrict someone or something within certain limits (space, scope or time)' - according to the Oxford dictionary.

People have a tendency to get mistaken by thinking that they have a relationship with God and they only have an acquaintance with him, and they wonder why situations or relationships never pan out for them. To have a solid relationship in any walk of life you need to have a relationship with the Most High. People think that hearing a word is enough to build a relationship; by only hearing a word you are introduced to him ,so in a sense he is an acquaintance. It is on your shoulders to change that 'acquaintance' status to a relationship by implementing time in your life to make time to mediate on his word - ensuring that you listen to hear and eyes are open to see the visions that he will give you in time.

When we become believers and begin to follow Christ, it is almost a natural progression as a single spirit being to want to find a life partner who we can pray and join hands with in fellowship. At the start of your journey, you'll see other couples within church but you're more focused on finding out whom and what God is. As time progresses you'll want a partner. It's a natural human desire but if we do not seek God for His guidance on this desire we can sometimes fall short.

Genesis 2:18 - 'The Lord God said it is not good for man to be alone. I will make a helper suitable for him. (NIV)'

Even God saw that is it not good for us to be alone, before we as men even knew we were alone. God said he will make someone suitable for us therefore if we pray and trust in God He will give us a person who is suitable and complements us. I am so happy that in this age more and more young adults are choosing to get married, as there was a time where no one had an interest in taking that big step towards marriage. It was all about having a girlfriend and that's that or a baby mother and people were happy, but finally people are discovering the other half that will compliment them and help them to achieve all that they have required in life.

Hebrews 13:4 - 'Marriage should be honoured by all and the marriage bed kept pure for god will judge the adulterer and all the sexually immoral. (NIV)'

Marriage should be the upmost goal for everyone as it is pleasing to God, especially if both are believers. The hardest thing for any couple, even more so if you have given your life to God, is to refrain from sex. We are all human and we all get the human impulse and the sexual desire, but stronger is he that doesn't give in to it. The older generation would say that, even then sharing a bed with someone that you are not married to, can be seen as immoral as you are unknowingly promoting what God despises. Times have slightly changed because now couples live together before they get married, whereas back in their day you couldn't live with your partner unless you were married to them.

2 Corinthians 6:14 - 'Do not be yoked together with unbelievers for what do righteousness and wickedness have in common? Or what fellowship can light have with darkness? (NIV)'

Even people who call themselves Christians can be unequally yoked, as many are working for the enemy and they do not even know it. I believe that it is time to lose that preconception that, just because a man or woman is a minister, they cannot be uneven - be aware of the wolves in sheep's clothing. Submerge yourself in the Lord through prayer and fasting, and he will identify to you if that person is right for you or not.

1 Peter 5:8 - 'Be alert and sober of mind, Your enemy the devil prowls around like a roaring lion looking for someone to devour.'

Too often the shallow, hidden person within us manifests and we gravitate to a person due to their dress sense and smooth lyrics of the tongue, and neglect the person's heart or the strength of their faith and the deep root of their spirit. Too often, I have seen and heard of men and women who are supposed to be part of the church chase and stalk each other for only one goal and purpose; I'm sorry but it's true. They use Christ as a cover up and, when they get what they desire, the person is abandoned. A trail of heartache is left with the other person watching as they try to do to others in the church what has been done to them. Now they might even start questioning God saying "if this man/women is yours, why did you allow them to do this to me?" It happens out in the world all too often, so please do not think that I am saying that it only happens in church. In the world people still question God, even if they don't personally know him as if they think they are owed something.The hurt can now make them cold towards anyone that approaches them. They can be so dismissive that they miss out on what God has put in front of them to help them heal. They have now confined themselves due to experiences that they should not have got themselves into.

1 Corinthians 15:33 - 'Do not be misled. Bad company corrupts good character. (NIV)'

At times, God will lead us to a person who is outside of the church and that doesn't make them any less than a person in church. We get so caught up in the idea of finding someone in church. We can miss what is in front of us and what has been planned for us by God because of our judgemental ideas. How do you know that a man or woman we come across is not already put there by God? He has already put things in order for us. Maybe they are there to give you a different view point or and different ideas that will only enhance you?

God sees you both as an unbreakable union. God may use either one of you so that you can show the other person something that they have never experienced before, giving them direction in the way of the Lord. He has probably been trying to reach them but because they are so engulfed in the world their spiritual ears are not hearing - they are lost.

Discovering a person that will complement us can be difficult, as we battle between the desires of the flesh and the requirements of the Spirit. Desires are the objects that we lust after. We can live without a desire; desires can be seen as a want. You can always do without a want but a requirement is a need. A need is something that we have to have to sustain ourselves for example, we need oxygen to survive and without it we would perish. So a requirement of a spirit is God and in God we receive spiritual growth.

Ecclesiastes 4:9-12 (ESV) - 'Two are better than one, because they have a good reward for their toil. For if they fall, one will lift up his fellow. But woe to him who is alone when he falls and has not another to lift him up! Again, if two lie together, they keep warm, but how can one keep warm alone? And though a man might prevail against one who is alone, two will withstand him—a threefold cord is not quickly broken.'

When I first started dating my wife, I was not in church, I was in the world. I used my faith as a side piece, only called on it when I was in a situation. Through her insisting on certain requirements that she needed, I had to change. She was a desire, a want that I wanted in my life - I had to change. I had to make the Lord a requirement in my life, not a side piece. I had to require him just as much as I require oxygen to breathe and, in turn, he made my wife a requirement and just not a desire. As the above scripture states at the end, three strands is not quickly broken with God as the binding agent in the relationship we cannot be easy broken when those around us, behind the scenes, might want us to fail.

No denomination, just togetherness in Christ

What is the meaning of the word 'denomination?' It means a recognized autonomous branch of the Christian Church. Denomination, I like to describe it as a guitar as there are many different makes but at the end of the day no matter the make it is still a guitar, no matter what stamp you up on it. *John 3:16* is one of the most iconic verses in the entire Bible, showing that God willingly gave his son knowing that through him we would have everlasting life. It wasn't for us to understand, but he had already set out a foundation, a blueprint for us to have access to his Holy Spirit. With this in mind, we should be united as one in his church as we all believe in what this verse says: that God gave his son and if you believe in Him, you will have everlasting life. He didn't say to follow Methodist teaching or Pentecostal teaching and so and so and you will have everlasting life. We all believe in Jesus walking in a straight direction, but the blinkers we have on are keeping us from being together.

This whole concept of denomination has always had me intrigued for years. When I first attended church, growing up in a Roman Catholic Church it was all I knew. I never knew there was anything called denomination almost as if I was in a bubble. I never knew the concept of denomination, to me church was just church. I never saw that there was a divide and separation. I'll talk more about the separation later in this chapter. When people use to ask me what denomination I was a part of, my response was always the same: "what is a denomination?" Every time their reply was "do you go to a Pentecostal, Baptist, Methodist, 7th day Adventist?" Me being me I was shocked, because I never knew that so much existed.

When I see the word denomination I see divide, split, cracks. I see a system that is used to divide the church. I have never once seen in the Old Testament God mention that he wants denominations. I have never seen in the New Testament Jesus mention that we should follow the restrictions of a denomination. He only ever mentioned one Spirit, one God, one kingdom and his one church which allows us to once again to receive what was taken away from us because of the sin of Adam and Eve. What we receive again is the gift to continually dwell in the attendance of the Holy Spirit, so if Jesus intended there to be one church, where did all these so-called 'denominations' come from? The answer is 'man.' It's mentioned in the scripture:

Matthew 12:25 (ESV) - 'Knowing their thoughts, he said to them, "Every kingdom divided against itself is laid waste, and no city or house divided against itself will stand.'

Everyone within each 'division' talks about unity and togetherness, but how many of them, or even us, are truly living it? Until we come together as one, we will continue to ruin Christ's original plan for his church. That is why the enemy is having a field day in the church and people don't realise until churches close and there is inner turmoil. If you were united and not divided, there is no way satan could bring issues amongst you. The Methodist Church was started by John Wesley and others as a movement within the Church of England in the 18th century. The Baptist Church - depending on where you are in the world - it would have been started by a different man - in England it is stated as Thomas Helwys. The Pentecostal Church, the modern Pentecostal Church is stated to be started by Charles Fox Parham.

The 7th day Adventist Church is stated as coming from the

great disappointment, James and Ellen White. Just giving a brief background on the different denominations.

Romans 16:17(ESV) - 'I appeal to you, brothers, to watch out for those who cause divisions and create obstacles contrary to the doctrine that you have been taught; avoid them.'

These denominations are all started by man's reasoning. Why? Because they decided to follow a certain teaching of Christ and not fully recognise all of his teaching. By picking and choosing what we follow we have systematically made Jesus Church like a jigsaw puzzle, where parts are pieced together, but never put together to create the picture it was supposed to. With people refusing to enter another Church, due to the teaching and the following of that particular denomination, yet if a person was to pass - meaning die -

people will attend to pay their respects at the person's funeral, regardless of their denomination. Why doesn't it matter then? But it matters any other time. You are finding that, in this day and age, the younger generation are more willing to go to any other Church regardless of denomination. It might be that they have friends in different churches, or that they go around learning to play an instrument in church, which in turn enables them to enhance their gift.

When a person goes away to the other side what would you think Jesus would say, knowing that his wife - his Church - is divided and split? The kind of person that I am, it doesn't matter about the denomination, I will visit and go to any church regardless of the denomination. Why? Because I don't conform to a religious mind set. I don't see myself a part of a denomination or belonging to bricks and mortar - I see myself as a spiritual person that God breathed life into when we were just dust, and the church I am a part of is Jesus Christ's church.

We need to get Christ's church united again as He is one body, one blood, one Spirit and do away with this created ideal of denomination. While we still hold onto this ideal we can never truly be united in Christ, and people wonder so many young men and women are leaving his church for earthly religions. Have you ever thought why this is happening? If not I'll tell you. It's because they feel a sense of brotherhood and a sense of togetherness under one roof.

1 Corinthians 12:28 (KJV) - 'And God hath set some in the church, first apostles, secondarily prophets, thirdly teachers, after that miracles, then gifts of healings, helps, governments, diversities of tongues.'

Let's be honest within each denomination. God is working, but can you imagine what it would be like if we took of the shackles of denomination and free ourselves mentally from that manmade idea, and instead strived for and gain a mentally of ONE GOD ONE CHRIST ONE CHURCH? How amazing it would be to have God's people united in the one Spirit and not separated in the ideas and fellowship of teaching of man. To move forward, we need to break the manmade chains of old and create new bonds/cords with Jesus Christ in the fellowship and brotherhood without restriction. Togetherness means 'the state of being close to another person or other people.' That's taken from the Oxford dictionary. If Christ has granted us salvation in him and we come together with an objective of needing to worship and praise then we should not allow sanctions of old to stop to us from achieving Christ's equitable place for us. Jesus wanted us to reach out to others and praise and worship God through

Him. He gave us the blueprint for it, but somewhere down the line people started to add to the blueprint to please themselves ultimately, and it leaves us in this situation. Once we enter into Christ, we are no longer strangers but citizens with GOD *(Ephesians 2:19-22.)* Here is one of the many hallmarks in the Bible that tells us instructions on how we need to be living and how we need to be and how to be thinking.

1 Corinthians 1:10-16 - In the scripture, you can see that there is already a divide amongst the people and Paul writes that there is already division as people are following the teaching of man and not Christ. So over 2000 plus years ago, people where already creating divisions and to this date it still appears. The question that we need to be asking ourselves is if it is men who created these denominations, did they bring me salvation or was it Christ who died for my sins? I will leave you with this last scripture just for you to think about. If you are receiving any of what is written in it, then is time to get united and do away with denominations and divisions:

Philippians 2:1-2 (NIV) - 'Therefore if you have any encouragement from being united with Christ, if any comfort from his love, if any common sharing in the Spirit, if any tenderness and compassion, ² then make my joy complete by being like-minded, having the same love, being one in spirit and of one mind.'

Building an atmosphere

'Atmosphere' can be described as the pervading tone or mood of a place, situation, or creative work. How I describe an atmosphere is creating an environment for the presence of the Lord to be present, so his Spirit can to begin to start His creative work.

2 Corinthians 10 3-5 New International Version (NIV) - 'For though we live in the world, we do not wage war as the world does. The weapons we fight with are not the weapons of the world. On the contrary, they have divine power to demolish strongholds. We demolish arguments and every pretension that sets itself up against the knowledge of God, and we take captive every thought to make it obedient to Christ.'

To be in an atmosphere is to distance one from the earthly things. In our homes it is to create a place (atmosphere) where the Holy Spirit can dwell. Many times do we pray and ask God for things, but we do not give Him the environment for him to work in, then we wonder why it's hard at times to make a connection with Him. By praising, we begin to tear down strong holds of the adversary; as these strong holds are broken down and destroyed, the Holy Spirit is able to enter and create new bonds and chains that can never be broken. Purge your household with prayer and/or praise and worship and allow God to have access, as he won't move within us without permission. Play gospel music; pray - if you play an instrument, play it in praise to the Lord. **Psalms 150:1-6** tells us how we ought to praise Him. There are so many ways that we can. What might be just noise to others is, in the presence of the Lord, praise to His ears. Praise Him without shame of who is watching. What you cannot see are that things you have asked for are already in preparation.

Jeremiah 33:3 (KJV) - 'Call unto me, and I will answer thee, and show thee great and mighty things, which thou knowest not.'

Switch off the TV, read a Psalm; listen to gospel - focus on the Lord...make that time in your day and give it to the Lord. It can be easy for us to get ourselves into a routine with the fast pace lifestyle that we all live, but a moment out to give to the Lord is how we stabilise our relationship with God and strengthen the bonds that we have created with Him, and it enables us to hear from God. Time taken to appreciate all he has done for you.

Colossians 3:16 (KJV) - 'Let the word of Christ dwell in you richly in all wisdom; teaching and admonishing one another in psalms and hymns and spiritual songs, singing with grace in your hearts to the Lord.'

There is nothing like dwelling in the presence of the Lord, having a connection with Him, having his grace fill you up. Have you ever created or been in atmosphere and just felt overwhelmed by the grace of God? Troubles that troubled you no longer trouble you - the weights on your shoulders are lifted and you feel free. What a mighty God we serve, He is mighty beyond what we can comprehend, so why would you not make time for him, as he is the way, the light and the truth?

An example of building an atmosphere in the Bible is Paul and Silas in *Acts 16:16.* While in prison they began to pray and sing song hymns. The power of the Lord worked in the prison; they felt an earthquake and the prison doors flew open.

Seeing and hearing this, the prison guard fell to his knees wanting to follow the ways of Jesus Christ. I find this to be a perfect example that when we have faith in our Lord God and we give him an atmosphere to work in - his ability and his power is endlessly at work. You don't need musical instruments to play, just open your mouth and sing onto him rejoice, shout and pray, let yourself go - release yourself from the conservative nature that we give ourselves, but be free without restricting yourself. Even if you think that you cannot sing, open your mouth and sing. If you are blessed to play an instrument play it, but play it with everything you have just don't go through the motions. You cannot expect all from God and only give him half of what you're supposed to give him.

We need to get past the physical praise and enter a state where our spirit begins to praise. Allow your spirit to raise and give praise as you start building an atmosphere. Through any sort of praise it begins with a physically praise, as the atmosphere is not yet right. We begin with a battle - a spiritual battle - that will either affect you in one or two ways. First, your mind might wonder on matters that it doesn't need to be thinking on at this moment in time. Secondly, distractions around you will disrupt what you're trying to achieve. If you can focus on your goal of connecting with God spiritually, then the atmosphere changes and your spirit raises up the tone in your praise. Things will change as you praise spiritually, and the Holy Spirit shifts and changes everything around you.

John 4 24 (NIV) - 'God is spirit, and his worshipers must worship in the Spirit and in truth.'

Why do you think in almost every church they have praise and worship at the start of the service? It is to create an atmosphere for the Holy Spirit to enter the building and for us to be in the presence of God. At times it is smooth, and the Holy Spirit of the Lord enters and rages through from the start of the service to the end, and people leave knowing that God presence within the atmosphere. We need to understand that it is not all plain sailing, and the enemy will try to do everything he can in his power to try and stop us getting to the place where we can be in God's company. Many times, we have Praise and Worship to begin the service and it is a battle. The atmosphere is uneasy at times, and it takes time for the person who is giving the word that day to finally allow that shift to happen.

My personal experience of this is the day of my baptism. The praise and worship team are in gear, raising songs and getting everyone singing; but the atmosphere was strange and though everyone was singing, a spiritual battle had started unbeknown to everyone in the building. The tide turned when the elders began to give testimony and encouragement to us, and it was at this point God said, "Enough is enough" and switched the atmosphere. You could feel the change in the atmosphere and God, through the person who gave the word after the testimonies, delivered a message through him and it put the final stamp on the evening.

Ephesians 6- 12 (KJV) - 'For we wrestle not against flesh and blood, but against principalities, against powers, against the rulers of the darkness of this world, against spiritual wickedness in high places.'

1 Peter 5 6-7 (NIV) - 'Humble yourselves, therefore, under God's mighty hand, that he may lift you up in due time. [7] Cast all your anxiety on him because he cares for you.'

The next verse talks about how the enemy plans to destroy us, but we have to stand firm within our faith and we shall overcome. The battle is never ending, especially when you are within the world. When you decide that the world is no longer for you, it is only his majesty and grace can fill and comfort you.

The key is preparation; you never put a cake into a cold oven. You always preheat the oven to give the cake the correct atmosphere for it to bake. For far too long, we have seen ourselves as the cake and the church as the oven, but we need to switch our mindset completely. We are the oven and the church, the building, is the cake. Prepared and already hot, it gives the church the right atmosphere for God to reside in the building. God breathed life into man, not into bricks and mortar. You can go church and, if you are not prepared, you might find that you leave not feeling anything. You leave the same way you entered, or you leave questioning your preacher's word or you are in a battle, in a struggle. Cold entering cold can never bring warmth, but warmth entering cold will bring warmth.

Push where possible to always have an atmosphere away from the earthly world we live in, to a place where God will move freely and without restriction, if we give him the right atmosphere to do so.

Learn to forgive

This can be very touch and go, meaning it is easy for us to walk away from a person or a situation. When a person has done us wrong, we ex communicate that particular person from ourselves and continue living with a hidden hatred for that person. Even when we think we are over it, a memory, a general everyday conversation can bring that hatred to the surface. It may start off as an innocent conversation but as it progresses the emotions of the past that were never conquered manifest, and it affects us emotionally. We can never truly understand why the hurt and pain of the past still have a hold on us like a straitjacket, as if the person is still pulling on the restraints, making it tighter and tighter. What we all desire is a release from the pain, and we distract ourselves by taking our mind off the issue be it by drinking, partying, smoking or making new friends; but ultimately, you have only covered it up. As if you have papered a wall but haven't dealt with the cracks in the wall. It looks pretty once it's papered, but the cracks remain as unseen. It may never be seen until you remove the paper, but the cracks can get wider and now the paper can longer hide it - and it appears for everyone to see. This is what we do when we cover things and never deal with them, but there is always a time when you have to deal with them - whether you like it or not.

The only way to move forward is to truly forgive the person for the wrongs that they have done. Saying you forgive a person is easy for some and they move on, but for others it's a lot harder. Those that find it hard either cut the person off completely but still hold resentment, or they say the words, "I forgive you," but they never truly do. To truly forgive is to speak it into being, but to also feel it within your spirit.

I myself have had to learn this. I had an experience while driving home, enjoying praise and worship when God spoke to me and said to move forward in my spiritual journey, I need to forgive those people in my past. I replied "I have forgiven them." God said, "No. You need to truly forgive them." At that moment, my spirit began to weep with all the hurt I had experienced in my life, the junk that I thought I was over was just embedded in me, like an emotional tidal wave. I began to pray but it wasn't helping, as I uttered the name of an individual that had caused me hurt followed by 'I FORGIVE YOU.' The emotional rage that was upon me began to ease. During that drive home, I truly forgave everyone that had hurt me and the hidden emotional straitjacket that they had on me was no more. I was finally released to move forward - even more in the direction that God needed me to follow and walk.

Why do we find it so hard to forgive, when it was easy for Christ to forgive us and say, "Forgive them father for they know not what they do?" Jesus had been tortured, humiliated, was practically at death's door - with the few words that He had in Himself, He still found the strength to forgive. Imagine if He hadn't asked for our forgiveness. Imagine if God released Him from the cross and never heard Jesus' plea to God to forgive us? God could have so easily destroyed man for what we did to his son. The thought of it should motivate you to truly forgive individuals in your past and present. Through Jesus asking for God to forgive us, rising from the grave and giving us access to the Holy Spirit, we have a connection to the Most High and the ability to tap into the gifts of heaven.

Yes, we know that words can be more harmful than the sword, as it can be easier to forgive someone who has physically harmed you than it can if they have used words to hurt and harm you. It most definitely is not easy to truly forgive, and one major factor could be our pride. We need to, at that instance of accepting and forgiving, diminish our pride. Allow this chain to be void from your temple. Pride is one of our trapdoors which we have as human beings. Pride is something that will keep us back, keeping us from achieving the gifts we are supposed to tap into and the blessings we are to achieve, once the true work of God has begun.

Proverbs 16:5 (NKJV) - 'The LORD detests all the proud of heart. Be sure of this: They will not go unpunished.'

One key aspect of forgiveness that we all know, is that God will forgive us our sins if and when we bring them to Him with a sincere heart. It clearly doesn't matter if you have been following Him for 6 months or 10 years. We all run to Him for forgiveness; we all seek forgiveness on our journey. As we walk on our journey, we need to realise that forgiveness is a key part of our faith and fellowship. Some of us don't realise it, but it's written in the Lord's Prayer. Yes that's right - the Lord's

Prayer that many of us recite everyday until the words become the norm. The sentences that I am referring to are: "forgive us our trespasses as we forgive those who trespass against us." I pose a question: if we don't forgive others, can we truly expect God to forgive our sins? Not allowing ourselves to forgive can become poison to our soul, as you become bitter and resentful. It is written in:

Mark 11:25 (NIV) - 'And when you stand praying, if you hold anything against anyone, forgive them, so that your Father in heaven may forgive you your sins.'

The above scripture proves that God, through Jesus, left instructions not for other's sake, but for the sake for our own salvation. We are quick to condemn the sinner, but the sinner seeks forgiveness just as much as we do.

Ephesians 4:32 - 'And be kind to one another, tenderhearted, forgiving one another, even as God in Christ forgave you.'

Forgiving is not saying the words, then a few weeks or months later you bring the situation back up. It's letting your forgiveness demonstrate itself, without reminiscing and gravitating to past emotions. It's about seeing, healing and learning.

Jesus said in *Matthew 18:21-22* that we should forgive a person seventy times seven. Seems an impossible task, but it is really? Is negativity an emotion of Christ? No it's not, so release yourself from the bondage that others have created within you. Countless scriptures teach us this, but as always, we pick and choose which one we follow and embed into the lifestyle that we live.

Luke 6:27 (NIV) - 'But to you who are listening I say: Love your enemies, do good to those who hate you, bless those who curse you, pray for those who mistreat you. Proverbs 10:12 (KJV) Hatred stirreth up strifes: but love covereth all sins.'

There is a whole paragraph in **2 Corinthians** that states that we should forgive the offenders. It starts from chapter 2 verse 5. **Psalms 130** shows us that we cry out for the Lord knowing that his forgiveness will bring us reverence - waiting on him longer than the watchman; knowing that his promises never fail but always come through. As we hold onto the animosity, the devil is able to creep in and slowly have his way with us. We fail to realise that we are slipping out of the ways of the Lord. Due to it being an emotion, we do not take it as seriously as we ought to. It can be the small things that we overlook that can slip us out of favour.

I will leave you with this statement:

How can you truly serve God with animosity in your heart?

LEARN TO FORGIVE.

Final thoughts

How many of us have been on our own journey in life, only to discover it is only when God moves within us and we accept Jesus Christ that we feel complete and our journeys become that much sweeter? We can lose those we first thought we were close to, once we accept Jesus as our Lord and saviour. That's because they are dead weight. They are the ones that have no place. They are the ones we relied on before God came and gave us something different, something that most of us will continue to search for. Searching in all the wrong places, thinking we have found what we are missing, but in reality all we have found is a dead end.

No matter how we try and fight it, once God has put us on our journey, we will finish that journey. We can try and divert from it thinking we know best, but ultimately when He says, "enough is enough," He will put things in place to direct us back on that path that we should have been travelling on. Have you ever been doing work or something in your life and felt that you have wanted more, felt that you needed fulfilment? Have you ever heard that voice that told you to go right, but you always turned left?

I find myself compelled with the thought that God has a plan for me; a plan waiting to take place, once I accept him as my Lord and Saviour. The Bible states that He knew us before we were even born and he has a plan for us. The roads we travel on are our choice. The gift we were given was the gift of free will - something that the angels were never given. We have a choice, the choice to walk God's path or be misled, like many of God's people by satan. It is amazing that, no matter what path we take, He is always with us and He is always waiting for us - watching and seeing if we are being attentive to His signs to return to him before it's too late.

He gives us chance after chance like an ever loving parent. We travel on a journey, thinking we are alone, but we are far from it; for if we walk by faith, not by sight our journey will be the sweetest we have ever known.

The Parable of the Lost Sheep - *John 15*

The Parable of the Sower - **Matthew 13**

You can stay out of fellowship if you wish, but the growth you may experience within it is greater than not being in it. Fellowship can help you to find out your purpose, fellowship can make you connect with people you thought you would never connect with. Just because you're new to fellowship doesn't mean you are the student, but you can also be a teacher bringing new ideas, new viewpoints and new understanding.

Just like stolons, sometimes the main plant is not on firm, fertile ground, but it is still able to spread its stems. Does that mean the other stems that branch out will be weak like the main one? The answer is 'no,' as one might end up in fertile ground and then that one takes over and begins to help feed plus sustain the other stems. Have you never seen when one family member finds God and it starts a chain reaction in that household?

Some of us are deep rooted within the church. We have parents that go, so we go living and following that path like our parents. I like to use the example: some of us are like stolons plants - an example of these types of plant would be strawberries. From a main plant they spread out - sometimes on fertile ground, sometimes on inadequate ground. Being like this has its good and bad nature; how may you ask the good nature is? You are still connected to the main plant. If you are on fertile ground, the stem that is created is able to spread also on fertile land and what you sowed you will reap in abundance. Using an example in church, we can see families that have been in the same church for generations. One side, they are on fertile ground and each generation grows better than the last, even sometimes spreading out into other churches and bringing that fullness with them. The bad side is that they can be connected to the main plant, but their personal ground is not on fertile ground. You can't create your own roots; you feed and sustain yourself from the main plant. This to me is an example of children and young adults who are made to go to church by their families, but they don't want to be there so they don't connect with God - just feed off the salvation of parents or relatives that bring them.

Your journey is taken and embarked upon by you. The experiences you have will either make you, or make you stumble - but never forget God almighty is always with you. The Bible holds the key to a successful and fulfilled journey. I hope that this book will help you to engage in dialogue with each other. Jesus is the blueprint, the Bible is the manual. For some, you might be living out one of many of the topics. I pray that they will help and guide you, understand that it is not of our understanding, but of the understanding of God and He will never lead you astray...so stand firm and stay blessed and stay humble.

1 Corinthians 2:9 - 10 (NIV) - 'However, as it is written:" What no eye has seen, what no ear has heard, and what no human mind has conceived the things God has prepared for those who love him - these are the things God has revealed to us by his Spirit. The Spirit searches all things, even the deep things of God.'